The Running Fox

In a place not far away

Past the woods on the edge of today,

Right beneath the Oaks

And left for years and years.

Through hedges of Hawthorn

And fields of gold

Beneath skies that will never grow old,

There runs a fox.

With a swish of her tail, a jump and a hop

She dreamed of a café, somewhere to stop.

She raced over fields and leapt over streams

From Longframlington to Longhoughton

From Felton to Kirkharle

"Let's bake some cakes!" She shouted with glee,

"Fluffy and sweet, as sweet as can be!

And sandwiches stacked, with fillings galore,

I'll invite all my friends – oh, what fun it will be."

She mixed up the batter

Her heart, open wide

"Chocolate or vanilla?" She pondered aloud,

A drizzle of lemon

Some caramel and cream

Carrots and walnuts

Oh, what a dream.

There are shortbreads and sponges

With chocolate and fudge,

There are quiches and pies

Warm and full of love.

The birds chirped a tune

And the people all danced

The tables were set

All were entranced

At the sandwiches layered, and cakes standing tall,

The café was ready

Come one, come all

The café was bright

With a cheerful sign…

"Delicious delights, come drink and dine!"

They peeked through the window,

Eyes wide with glee,

At cakes piled high, as sweet as can be.

"Please, Running Fox, may I have a bite?

A sandwich or a scone, what a delight!"

She whipped up a sandwich

And melted some cheese

"Could I have some Tuna and tomato, please"

Then a Bakewell appeared

With a cherry on top

They all squealed with joy

They could hardly stop

With treats piled high

In a hamper, so neat,

Some sat outside

Took the weight off their feet

Under the blue sky

Shared with friends

A picnic with laughter

Where joy never ends

So, should you wander

Where the wildflowers play

Look for the fox

With cakes on display,

The café is open

The doors open wide

Stay for a while

Step inside.

Printed in Great Britain
by Amazon